D0459226

97
00

1970—1979

Yearbooks in Science

1970–1979

GERALDINE MARSHALL GUTFREUND

Twenty-First Century Books
A Division of Henry Holt and Company
New York

Twenty-First Century Books
A Division of Henry Holt and Company, Inc.
115 West 18th Street
New York, NY 10011

Henry Holt® and colophon are trademarks of
Henry Holt and Company, Inc.
Publishers since 1866

Library of Congress Cataloging-in-Publication Data
Yearbooks in science.
p. cm.
Includes indexes.
Contents: 1900–1919 / Tom McGowen—1920–1929 / David E. Newton—1930–1939 / Nathan Aaseng—1940–1949 /
Nathan Aaseng—1950–1959 / Mona Kerby—1960–1969 / Tom McGowen—1970–1979 / Geraldine Marshall
Gutfreund—1980–1989 / Robert E. Dunbar—1990 and beyond / Herma Silverstein.
ISBN 0–8050–3431–5 (v. 1)
1. Science—History—20th century—Juvenile literature. 2. Technology—History—20th century—Juvenile literature.
3. Inventions—History—20th century—Juvenile literature. 4. Scientists—20th century—Juvenile literature.
5. Engineers—20th century—Juvenile literature. [1. Science—History—20th century. 2. Technology—History—
20th century.]
Q126.4.Y43 1995
609'.04—dc20   95–17485
                                                                                                                 CIP
                                                                                                                 AC

ISBN 0–8050–3437–4
First Edition 1995

Printed in Mexico
All first editions are printed on acid-free paper ∞.
10 9 8 7 6 5 4 3 2 1

Cover design by James Sinclair
Interior design by Kelly Soong

Cover photo credits
Background: Tree destroyed by acid rain, © John Shaw/Tom Stack & Associates. **Inset images** (clockwise from top
right): *E. coli* bacteria, © David Phillips/Photo Researchers, Inc.; Earth Day banner created by James Sinclair; Fractal
design, © David Young/Tom Stack & Associates; Chimpanzee, Reuters/Bettmann; Tube worms, Dudley Foster/Woods
Hole Oceanographic Institution; *Voyager* mission patch, NASA.

Photo credits
p. 10: UPI/Bettmann; p. 11 (left), p. 12: John Reader/Science Photo Library/Photo Researchers, Inc.; p. 11 (right): ©
Tom McHugh/Science Source/Photo Researchers, Inc.; p. 15: © Francois Gohier/Photo Researchers, Inc.; p. 20: (left)
Rod Catanach/Woods Hole Oceanographic Institution, (right) J. Frederick Grassle/WHOI; p. 21, 38: UPI/Bettmann
Newsphotos; p. 25: A. B. Dowsett/SPL/Photo Researchers, Inc.; p. 26: UPI/Bettmann; p. 27, 51: Dr. Rob
Stepney/SPL/Photo Researchers, Inc.; p. 28, 41, 57: © Will and Deni McIntyre/Photo Researchers, Inc.; p. 33: David
Parker/ESA/SPL/Photo Researchers, Inc.; p. 40: Thomas Kitchin/Tom Stack & Associates; p. 42: Tony
Craddock/SPL/Photo Researchers, Inc.; p. 46: (left) © Hank Morgan/Photo Researchers, Inc.; (right, top, & bottom) ©
David Young/Tom Stack & Associates; p. 48: American Institute of Physics/Niels Bohr Library/Marshak Collection; p.
53: U.S. Library of Congress/Mark Marten/Photo Researchers, Inc.; p. 61: NASA/Tom Stack & Associates; p. 62: Max
Plack Institut fur Extraterrestrische Physik/SPL/Photo Researchers, Inc.; p. 64: NASA/Mark Marten/Photo
Researchers, Inc.; p. 65: NASA; p. 66: NASA/JPL/TSADO/Tom Stack & Associates; p. 69: (right & left) Airworks/Tom
Stack & Associates.

In memory of my father, Clifton J. Marshall, who shared with me his love of libraries, books, and chocolate malts; and for my children, Audrey and Rachel, who share with me their books—and their chocolate malts.

Acknowledgments

The author wishes to extend special thanks to Caroline L. Herzenberg of Argonne National Laboratory, Dr. Carolyn Green, Cal Sisto, R. Mike Mullane, Vera Rubin, Christine B. Campbell of the Association for Women in Science, and Phillip F. Schewe of the American Institute of Physics for interviews and research information. Extra thanks go to Mona and Al Proctor for lots of computer help!

Contents

1

ARCHAEOLOGY, ANTHROPOLOGY, AND PALEONTOLOGY

Anthropology is the study of human beings and their culture. Archaeology is the study of past cultures through their remains, including fossils, monuments, and those things that the people used in their daily lives. Paleontology is the study of the past through fossils. A paleoanthropologist is a scientist who studies the fossils of hominids—humans, including those species that came before us, and their close evolutionary relatives. These fields are closely related and discoveries are often the result of scientists from the different fields working together, along with other scientists, such as geologists.

The decade of the 1970s was an important time of discovery, especially about two life-forms that will always fascinate people—people themselves and their ancestors, and the beings that ruled the earth before us, dinosaurs.

FACES OF FORGOTTEN ANCESTORS

One of the most important areas where discoveries of fossils of the earliest species of humans and their ancestors have been made in the twentieth century is the Great Rift Valley in Africa.

In 1924, Raymond Dart, a young anatomy professor, discovered the skull of an early hominid, *Australopithecus africanus*. This skull became known as the Taung child. Then, in 1959, a husband and wife team of paleoanthropologists, Louis and Mary Leakey, discovered another early hominid, later referred to as *Australopithecus robustus*. They nicknamed their find Zinjanthropus, or "Zinj." In the 1960s, the Leakeys' son Jonathan found the first fossils from a species that Louis Leakey named *Homo habilis*, meaning "handy man." But there was disagreement over whether this species was truly the first human species, as Louis Leakey believed it was.

In 1972, Jonathan's brother, Richard Leakey, found a fragmented skull, known as 1470, which he identified as *Homo habilis*. The Leakeys believed this skull proved the early existence of a human species, and they believed the skull to be almost 3 million years old. Louis Leakey died of a heart attack soon after its discovery and so did not live to see the controversy erupt yet again over who had found the earliest ancestor of modern humans. Dating methods other than the one used by the Leakeys identified 1470 as only approximately 1.9 million years old. No matter how old it was, 1470 was an important find, for what it could tell us about *Homo habilis*.

Rarely are the fragments of a complete skull found—1470 was an exception. It took Maeve Leakey (Richard's wife) five weeks to piece it together. Maeve was quoted in Richard Leakey's and Roger Lewin's book *People of the Lake* as saying, "I always liked jigsaws, and as a child, I used to turn them upside down if I found them too easy."

Richard and Maeve Leakey, with a thighbone and the reconstructed skull of the hominid called 1470

This find is a good example of the fact that scientists sometimes disagree and that new technology and new discoveries can change what is believed. Even newer techniques in dating fossils such as 1470, as well as new fossil finds, may yet change our picture of our ancestors, but each new piece of the puzzle leads us closer to a more complete whole. Science is not something that never changes. It can always teach us new things—even about the past.

THE LOVELY LUCY

One of the most important discoveries of the 1970s was made in 1974 in Ethiopia, by paleoanthropologist Donald Johanson. Described in his book with James Shreeve, *Lucy's Child: The Discovery of a Human Ancestor*, Dr. Johanson's discoveries actually began in 1973 when, just out of graduate school, after weeks of having "scrambled around in the stifling heat" looking for hominids that "were keeping themselves well hidden," he uncovered a hominid knee joint that showed that human ancestors walked upright almost 3½ million years ago.

Then, on November 30, 1974, Dr. Johanson discovered "what appeared to be a fragment of an elbow joint." Unbelievably, he next saw a femur (a leg bone), a piece of pelvis, ribs, and some vertebrae. As he and his colleagues put the bones together, Dr. Johanson saw that he had discovered a nearly complete skeleton of a 3½-foot- (1-meter-) tall female hominid about the size of a chimpanzee. The hominid was named Lucy, after a song by the Beatles, "Lucy in the Sky with Diamonds," which was playing in Johanson's camp on

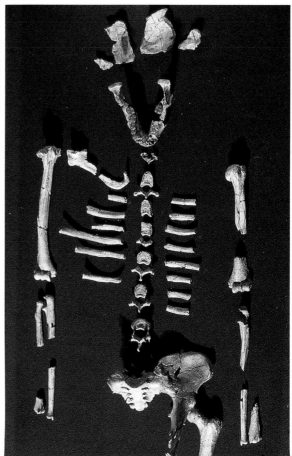

Above: *Donald Johanson*
Right: *Lucy, the fossil skeleton discovered by Donald Johanson*

the day the skeleton was excavated. He wrote, "We all shared the feeling that this ancient creature was being re-created, coming to life before our eyes. . . . Whatever she turned out to be, Lucy was sure to be one of the biggest finds of the century."

What she turned out to be, Dr. Johanson realized after much study of Lucy and of more fossils found in 1975, was "the common ancestor to all other known hominids." Dr. Johanson and his team had discovered a 3½-million-year-old, previously unknown hominid, which he named *Australopithecus afarensis.*

It is important to realize that not all scientists agreed with Dr. Johanson. Richard Leakey believed that the true ancestor of modern humans was yet to be found.

Many, though, believed that Lucy was the mother of humankind.

FOOTSTEPS FROM THE PAST

In 1978, a team led by Mary Leakey found a trail of footprints in the Laetoli beds, sedimentary areas in the country of Tanzania, in Africa's Great Rift Valley. The footprints had been made by human ancestors. The finding of these footprints shows the luck that is sometimes involved in discovering the distant past. The footprints were preserved because a volcano had sent down some ash three and a half million years ago. The ash was walked on, after some rain had fallen. When the rain made the volcanic ash wet, it produced a mineral crystal called trona, which hardens like concrete. Like the handprints of modern movie stars, the footsteps of our long-ago ancestors were preserved for future fans to gaze on in wonder.

The trail of hominid footprints fossilized in volcanic ash at Laetoli. The footprints are of two adults, with possibly a third set belonging to a child who walked in the footsteps of one of the adults.

DINOSAUR DISCOVERIES

People's fascination for those ancient dragons, the dinosaurs, began in 1677 when a chemistry professor at Oxford University in England found a huge bone, which he identified as belonging to a giant. The quest to discover more about these giant reptiles, rulers of the earth before they vanished sixty-five million years ago, was an active one in the decade of the 1970s.

ARCHAEOLOGY BY ACCIDENT

Not all archaeological and paleontological discoveries are made by scientists. George E. Stuart, an archaeologist with the National Geographic Society, says that "many discoveries, often valuable ones, are made by accident." The 1970s held its share of archaeological finds by non-scientists:

- While moving earth for a new housing subdivision near the Black Hills in South Dakota in 1974, George Hanson discovered a number of bones 20 feet (6 meters) underground. Fortunately, Hanson's son told a former college professor about the bones. The professor realized that the bones were those of mammoths. The mammoths had died 26,000 years earlier.

- Also in 1974, workers digging a well on a commune in southeastern China were surprised to find large clay models of men's heads, arms, and bodies, as well as arrowheads. It is reported that children played with the clay pieces and that clay heads were offered for sale at roadside stands.

  Luckily, the workers told about their discovery at a commune meeting before much of the material was destroyed. When archaeologists excavated, they eventually found almost 7,500 figures of life-size clay horses and soldiers that had been made twenty-two centuries earlier. Each of the soldiers' faces is different, and scientists think they may have been modeled after real people. Looking as if ready to go into battle, the clay army had been made to guard the tomb of China's first emperor, Qin Shi Huangdi.

- In Mexico City, while digging a trench for an electric cable in 1978, workers found a stone disk with pictures of an Aztec moon goddess. Archaeologists dug farther and discovered an ancient Aztec city that had been buried for 400 years. In the temple of Huitzilopochtli, the skulls of thirty-four children who had been sacrificed to the rain god, Tlaloc, were discovered.

- In 1979, a crew of Chinese construction workers were digging for natural gas while building a factory. They dug up dinosaurs instead. The site, the Dashanpu quarry in Zigong, Szechwan, has proved to be one of the richest sources of dinosaur fossils in the world, revealing dinosaurs not found anywhere else on earth.

Paleontologists offered surprising theories and evidence that some dinosaurs may have been warm-blooded, a term meaning that an animal can help control its own body temperature instead of depending primarily on outside heat or cold. And, contrary to popular belief, some dinosaurs may actually have been good mothers.

THE MIGHTY *SUPERSAURUS*

Jim Jensen was quoted in the *New York Times* once as saying, "While some boys dreamed of a new bicycle, I dreamed of finding dinosaurs. I would always wake up before I could dig them up."

In 1972, Jensen was digging for dinosaurs in western Colorado when his son, Ron, uncovered an 80-foot- (24-meter-) long dinosaur shoulder blade. This turned out to have belonged to a dinosaur that scientists believe was between 82 and 98 feet (25 and 30 meters) long (perhaps as long as 140 feet, or 42 meters, including its tail), and 54 feet (16 meters) high—the biggest dinosaur yet discovered. Mr. Jensen named his discovery *Supersaurus*. *Supersaurus* would have been as tall as two giraffes standing one on top of the other, and as long as or even longer than a blue whale, the largest living mammal.

Jensen found a 10-foot- (3-meter-) long shoulder blade in 1979, which he thought belonged to a creature that he named *Ultrasaurus*. These animals would have been heavier but not necessarily longer than *Supersaurus*. But some scientists doubt that this bone really belonged to a new creature, and think the bone may actually have been part of an already known dinosaur, *Brachiosaurus*. Meanwhile, scientists have continued to search for the largest dinosaur of them all.

ARE DINOSAURS AND BIRDS RELATED?

While still a graduate student in 1975, dinosaur paleontologist Robert Bakker published an article in *Scientific American* that suggested that dinosaurs had a close relationship to birds. (Dr. Bakker has even written that "dinosaurs are alive today. We call them birds.") He also believed that at least some dinosaurs were warm-blooded.

Scientists still disagree today about how closely related birds are to dinosaurs. After a meeting in 1978 in which they exchanged information and

Robert Bakker, holding a cast of an Allosaurus *skull*

ideas, many scientists decided that smaller, active dinosaurs were probably warm-blooded and that larger dinosaurs were probably warmed by their own large, heavy bodies. But most felt that we'll never really know for sure.

Perhaps most importantly, as Don Lessem said in his book *Dinosaur Discoveries*, "Though it reached a dead end, the hot-blooded dinosaur debate captivated public interest anew in dinosaurs, revamped the animals' sorry image, and thereby helped bring a new generation of bright young minds into the science."

What Happened to the Dinosaurs?

Scientists are still debating the case of the disappearing dinosaurs today, but a discovery in 1977 by geologist Walter Alvarez gave them an important clue. In a sixty-six million-year-old layer of rock in Italy, he discovered iridium. Iridium is an element that exists in comets, meteors, and asteroids, as well as at the earth's core. Walter Alvarez believed that the iridium in the Italian rock showed that a giant object from space had hit the earth, close to the time when dinosaurs disappeared. Other iridium concentrations since found around the world give further clues that something *did* hit the earth sixty-five million years ago, transforming the home of the dinosaurs with carbon soot, fires, volcanic eruptions, and large temperature changes, creating a habitat that could no longer support them.

Other scientists disagree with this sudden extinction theory, believing in a more gradual extinction. But Walter Alvarez has said, "Dinosaurs did last for nearly 140 million years, and we believe that had it not been for the asteroid impact, they would still be the dominant creatures on earth."

What might the dinosaurs have become? One scientist has even guessed that dinosaurs would have eventually evolved into upright, human-like creatures!

GOOD MOTHER LIZARD

When he was eight years old, future paleontologist John R. "Jack" Horner found a dinosaur bone on his father's ranch. He has been fascinated with dinosaurs ever since. Specifically, Jack Horner is interested in duck-billed dinosaurs. In his book with James Gorman, *Digging Dinosaurs*, Dr. Horner explained that he had hunted for dinosaur fossils in Montana and Canada and that "duckbills were what I found, so duckbills were what I looked for." He wrote that scientific research is "like taking a tangled ball of twine and trying to unravel it," and that "dinosaurs were my ball of string. Duckbills were the only loose end that I had been able to find, so I had been tugging on them for all they were worth."

In 1978, on a dinosaur-hunting trip in Montana, Jack Horner untangled a big part of that ball of twine by finding the first known dinosaur eggs and nests in North America.

Dr. Horner's first clue about the dinosaur nests was not found in the field but in a small rock shop that had once been a church in the tiny Montana town of Bynum. There, he and his friend Bob Makela were shown two pieces of bone by the shop owner. Dr. Horner realized, "What I had in my hand was a bone from a baby dinosaur, a duckbill—exactly what I wanted, in a place I never expected to find it." The shop owner gave Jack Horner a coffee can full of other bones and told him where they had been found.

At the site, on a cattle ranch near Choteau, Montana, on August 9, 1978, Jack Horner and his friend found a dinosaur nest containing fossilized bones and eggshells. In this and other dinosaur nests, Dr. Horner discovered broken eggshells. This showed that the young had remained in the nest long enough to smash the shells. He found bones showing that the young were too undeveloped to fend for themselves right after birth. And he found fossilized food regurgitated by the parent dinosaurs that would have been given to the young. He realized that these dinosaurs probably tended to their babies much as modern birds do their young. Dr. Horner wrote that "the best way to grow like a bird is to be warmblooded like a bird."

Not only did his find indicate that these dinosaurs were warm-blooded, but as Dr. Horner said in his book, "This was the first time anyone had found a nest not of eggs but of baby dinosaurs, and the evidence seemed to me incontrovertible [indisputable] that these babies had to have stayed in that nest while they were growing and that one or more parents had to care for them. This kind of behavior, unheard of in dinosaurs, was probably the most startling discovery to come out of that dig. . . . It was in such severe contrast to the image of how dinosaurs were supposed to behave—laying eggs and leaving them, like turtles or lizards or most reptiles. If dinosaurs, even just some species of dinosaur, had acted like birds and reared their young in nests, caring for them and bringing them food, this was a bit of information that would profoundly change our sense of what sort of creatures these ancient reptiles were."

Jack Horner named his new species of dinosaur *Maiasaura peeblesorum*. *Peeblesorum* was in honor of the family who owned the land where the nests were found. *Maiasaura* was in honor of the mother dinosaur herself. It means "good mother lizard."

2

BIOLOGY AND MEDICINE

Biology is basically the study of living beings. The decade of the 1970s included some startling discoveries in marine biology, the study of the ocean's life; and in the field of zoology, the study of animals, a disturbing discovery was made about humankind's close cousins, the chimpanzees. Humans were also making amazing discoveries about themselves—how to engineer their own genes, and how to create a baby in a test tube. And scientists were beginning the research that would lead, in the 1980s, to the discovery of the most frightening disease of the twentieth century: AIDS.

LIFE AT THE BOTTOM OF THE SEA

Before 1977, scientists believed that there would be little animal life found in the dark waters at the bottom of the ocean. But on February 19, 1977, the research submarine the *Alvin*, dived 8,200 feet (2,460 meters) below the surface at the Galápagos Ridge, or Rift, 200 miles (320 kilometers) northeast of the Galápagos Islands in the Pacific Ocean. The sea had a surprise waiting for *Alvin*'s crew—giant 5-foot- (1.5-meter-) long red worms, worms about the size of a twelve-year-old boy or girl, encased in white tubes.

The crew of the *Alvin* also discovered deep-sea fish and unknown species of clams, mussels, crabs, and jellyfish. An oceanographer on board, John Corliss, recalled looking "out our ports [windows] to see shimmering water streaming up past the submarine with pink fish hovering in the warm water, white crabs scuttling over the rocks, huge white clams and yellow-brown mussels, and the long, white tubes of worms with red plumes."

Scientists discovered that in a rift, which is between two plates of the earth's crust, there are areas where seawater mixes with dissolved minerals. The minerals come from lava pushing up from below the crust. There is also

The deep-sea submarine Alvin *is launched from a research vessel.*

Tube worms were just one of the fabulous new life-forms discovered by the crew of the Alvin.

sulfur present, which scientists believe allows a certain kind of bacteria to live, forming the first link of the food chain for the amazing animals that have been found at the bottom of the sea.

CHIMPANZEES AT WAR

As a child, Jane Goodall hugged a chimpanzee doll and dreamed of going to Africa after reading the *Tarzan* and *Doctor Dolittle* books. She fulfilled her dream in 1960 when she arrived in Africa in Gombe, Tanzania, to study the wild chimpanzees. During the 1960s, she made the amazing discovery that chimpanzees both make and use tools. She discovered a chimp, one that she had named David Greybeard, stripping leaves off a twig and using it as a tool to fish termites from their tunnels. Of her first decade with the chimpanzees, Jane Goodall has said, "I thought how like people they [the chimps] were, but much nicer, kinder, gentler." But the decade of the seventies revealed a darker side to chimpanzee society.

In her book *Through a Window*, Dr. Goodall said that "1974 marked the start of 'the four-year war' at Gombe." The group of chimpanzees that Jane Goodall had been studying had by this time divided into two separate communities. The two communities were called the southern Kahama community and the northern Kasakela community. In 1974 "came the first brutal attack by Kasakela males on a Kahama male . . . when a Kasakela patrol of six adult males suddenly came upon the young male, Godi. . . . Humphrey was the first to grab Godi, seizing one of his legs and throwing him to the ground. Figan, Jomeo, Sherry and Evered pounded and stamped on their victim, while Humphrey pinned him to the ground, sitting on his head and holding his legs with both hands. . . . [Godi] undoubtedly . . . died of his injuries, for he was never seen again." After this first attack, one by one, all of the adult members of the Kahama community were hunted down and killed by the members of the Kasakela community. Such violent war has only been recorded in one other species of mammal: the human species.

Jane Goodall has said that it is sad and "a bit horrifying to consider that just because we now know how aggressive the chimpanzees can be, this makes . . . [them] . . . even more like humans than I thought."

Jane Goodall is shown here speaking at a fund-raiser, seeking to raise money to save the earth's wild primates, like the chimpanzee in the enlarged photo beside her.

But in her book, Jane Goodall went on to say, "Gradually, however, I learned to accept the new picture. For although the basic aggressive patterns of chimpanzees are remarkably similar to our own, their comprehension of the suffering they inflict on their victims is very different from ours. Chimpanzees, it is true, are able to empathize, to understand at least to some extent the wants and needs of their companions. But only humans, I believe are capable of *deliberate* cruelty—acting with the intention of causing pain and suffering."

HOW PEOPLE AND CHIMPANZEES ARE ALIKE

The ability to make and use tools, and the unfortunate ability to wage war, are not the only things that chimps and people have in common. Other common characteristics are:

- Similarities in brain structure and body chemistry. The blood of chimpanzees is so similar to human blood that people have been able to receive blood transfusions from chimps. Chimpanzees can also get some of the same diseases, such as polio, that people can.

- Chimpanzees comfort one another with hugs and may kiss and hug one another as a greeting, just as people do.

- Some scientists think that chimpanzees actually use medicine! Chimpanzees have been found to eat leaves of Aspilia plants, even though they don't seem to enjoy the taste and there is little food value in these leaves for the chimps. Some kinds of Aspilia leaves do contain an antibiotic, though, and the leaves are used by native African peoples for stomach problems, coughs, and fevers.

- Chimpanzees play games. One scientist has reported that at a zoo where an adult chimp had been bitten on his hand and stumbled around on his bent wrist, a number of the young chimps imitated him as a funny game to play with one another.

- Chimpanzees have learned how to communicate with humans and with one another using symbols, computers, and American Sign Language. They've even made up their own words! A chimp named Washoe called a fizzy soft drink a listen drink, using two signs that she knew. Washoe also came up with a new sign for one of her keepers, a man named George. In the early 1970s, George, as did many men, wore long hair. Washoe combined the sign for *g* with a movement stroked down the back of her head as if to imitate his long hair! Then, since George was often the person who got her breakfast, Washoe changed his sign name to a noisy slapping of her head so that she could get his attention. This worked so well that she was soon using it to get other people's attention. The scientists in the lab called this the Hey You! sign. Other chimpanzees picked up the Hey You! sign, using it with people and even with other chimpanzees.

Finding a Cure, or Creating Frankenstein's Monster?

The 1970s was an extremely important time in the development of genetic engineering. Scientists built on the discoveries of previous decades, such as the discovery that DNA held the hereditary code. At one time, scientists had felt that proteins held the blueprints of life. The structure of DNA had been discovered by scientists James Watson and Francis Crick in the 1950s, leading the way for scientists of the 1970s to learn how to actually change the DNA of plants and animals. There was a great deal of controversy regarding genetic engineering. The question in the public's mind was, are we finding a cure for diseases, or creating Frankenstein's monster?

Recombinant DNA

DNA (deoxyribonucleic acid) is basically an organism's blueprint or plan, a chemical substance that contains the instructions that determine what traits that organism inherits. These traits can include such things as eye color, hair color—and disease. Recombinant DNA is the combination of the DNA of two different organisms. The making of recombinant DNA in a laboratory is a major technique used in genetic engineering. The ability to make recombinant DNA enables scientists to make new gene combinations that do not naturally exist. Genetic engineering techniques allow scientists to create drugs, such as human insulin. Basically human insulin is made by inserting human insulin genes into bacteria that then reproduce quickly, reproducing the insulin at the same time. The insulin can then be given to diabetics. Other genetically engineered drugs include human growth hormone, hepatitis B vaccine, and a chemical that dissolves heart attack-causing blood clots. Genetic engineering is also useful in agriculture, to produce substances that can do such things as preventing frost from forming on potatoes and destroying them. Other benefits of genetic engineering for agriculture include improving livestock so that it is more disease resistant. In the 1990s, doctors are even beginning to find cures for genetic diseases in people; gene-altered cells are inserted into the body of a patient in the hope that these genes will cure his or her disease.

The technology that made these medical miracles possible was developed in the 1970s, but not easily and not without much controversy. While there is only room to mention the highlights of the decade's research with recombinant DNA here, it is important to realize that this work was the result of the contributions of many scientists. Some of these scientists were interested in basic research, which involves just knowing how things work, without a special plan for a product or cure in mind, and some were doctors who were desperately searching for a cure for ill patients. Both kinds of research are valuable. As molecular biologist and science writer Larry Thompson said in his book *Correcting the Code*, "The scientific community's article of faith said that discoveries by basic scientists about the fundamental processes of life often lead to something practical, such as a useful medical treatment."

TOBACCO WORMS HAVE TO EAT, TOO!

I didn't start out planning to be a writer. I graduated from college in 1977 with a degree in zoology, hoping perhaps to be the next Jane Goodall. Meanwhile, though, I needed to pay the bills and so I begged one of my former biology professors, Dr. Ray Hakim, for a job. Now, at that time, my visions of working in a lab involved spending my days in a place filled with the newest wonder equipment and scientists shouting, "Eureka! I have found the answer!" Dr. Hakim had such a lab in a new, tall research building and he may have even shouted "Eureka" now and then, but I soon discovered that even the most sophisticated lab needs something to experiment with and someone to take care of it. Dr. Hakim hired me to be that someone.

Dr. Hakim was studying cell division and he was working with an animal that had easy-to-study, slow-dividing cells. Those animals were big, green tobacco worms. (Actually, they were caterpillars, but no one ever called them that!) I worked in a very old building that seemed to be collapsing in shame across a path from the gleaming research building. My building was known to have rats as big as cats. I baked something that looked very much like granola bars, which the worms ate. I gathered the tobacco worm moths (which laid the eggs from which grew our worms) from an enormous, walk-in cage. If I went in at dusk, I came out with large brown moths covering the back of my white lab coat. Sometimes when I checked my worms in the morning, I found the big ones eating the small ones. I also found sick worms turning a lovely shade of black. I gave the sick and partly eaten worms a worm funeral by poking them into a big milk jug filled with alcohol.

I made all of $2.50 an hour at this job. I had a college degree in zoology, but jobs were so scarce in all fields of biology in the seventies, I was thrilled with the pay!

I have to admit that my favorite part of the job was when Dr. Hakim celebrated getting a research paper published by taking everyone out for pizza. It almost made up for the rats!

Without my care of the lowly tobacco worms, the whole lab, complete with its gleaming glass and electron microscopes, would have ground to a halt. But I tried not to let the importance of my job go to my head—especially since there might have been a moth sitting high on my head at the time.

Both kinds of research led to recombinant DNA and its uses—one of the most important advances of the twentieth century:

- A biochemist, Dr. Paul Berg, and his lab associates, working in the early part of the seventies, succeeded in combining DNA from different organisms for the first time. This DNA, created in the laboratory, became known as recombinant DNA. Dr. Berg is often called the father of genetic engineering.

- Molecular biologists Stanley Cohen and Herbert Boyer discovered genetic cloning in 1973, a way of inserting recombinant DNA into bacteria that would then make billions of identical copies of the gene.

- Throughout the 1970s, many people feared that reengineered genes could somehow escape the laboratory and infect people with new and incurable diseases. There were also fears that scientists would use the new genes to try to create an unnatural race of people—a race of super-people, or Frankenstein's monsters. While the potential for irresponsible people misusing this technology is something we must continue to monitor, the safekeeping of recombinant DNA molecules in the lab by responsible scientists was solved in 1975. Scientists created a weakened strain of *E. coli* bacteria that could not survive outside the laboratory. Since the bacteria that would hold the recombinant DNA could not survive outside the lab, there was no chance that it could escape into the world and accidentally infect anyone.

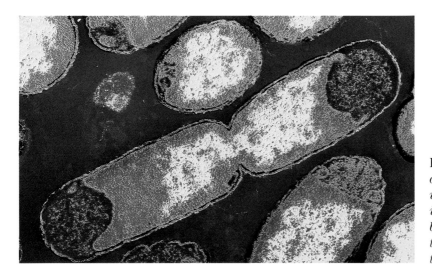

E. coli *bacteria, an organism commonly used in genetic engineering experiments, has been magnified thousands of times in this photograph.*

• Scientists announced that recombinant DNA techniques had produced the first genetically engineered drug, insulin, in 1978. People with Type I diabetes do not produce the hormone insulin in the pancreas and therefore cannot absorb sugar. They will die without insulin. Though many diabetics can inject insulin produced from animal pancreas, which has been available since the 1920s, some diabetics are allergic to insulin made from animals. But they can now take the human insulin made by recombinant DNA.

The supply of animal-produced insulin could run low with increasing demand by the year 2000, but the insulin created through recombinant DNA techniques could be continuously produced.

LITTLE MISS PERFECT

On July 25, 1978, a seemingly ordinary event—the birth of a 5-pound, 12-ounce (2.6-kilogram) baby girl—happened in Britain. But the birth of Louise Brown was announced by a frenzy of news headlines proclaiming her OUR MIRACLE BABY, BABY OF THE CENTURY, THE MIRACLE AT MIDNIGHT, and LITTLE MISS PERFECT. Louise Brown was the first baby conceived by in vitro (literally translated as "in glass") fertilization, meaning that she grew from an egg fertilized outside her mother's body.

Louise's mother had blocked fallopian tubes, which meant that her eggs could not be fertilized. This is a common problem when women cannot conceive a baby. But Louise's mother and father wanted a baby badly, so they went to a pair of scientists, Patrick Stepcoe, a physician, and Robert Edwards, a physiologist, for help.

The two researchers had been trying for over a decade to achieve a miracle child

Louise Brown and her parents made their American TV debut on the Donahue show in September 1979.

such as Louise. They had succeeded more than eighty times in removing eggs from women and fertilizing them with sperm in the lab, but each time the embryos were implanted back into a woman's uterus, the baby failed to develop. With Mrs. Brown, the scientists tried something different. They had always waited until the egg was about four and a half days old before, but this time, they tried implanting a younger embryo, one only about two and a half days old. And it worked! Dr. Edwards said, after Louise's birth, "The last time I saw the baby it was just eight cells in a test tube. It was beautiful then, and it's still beautiful now."

There was much debate concerning the first test tube baby. Some people felt that no one should tamper with nature, but Mrs. Brown disagreed. She described her daughter Louise, the first test tube baby, as "so small, so beautiful, so perfect."

A LOOK INSIDE THE BRAIN

New diagnostic machines, machines that could help a doctor find out what was wrong with a patient, were developed in the 1970s. They gave doctors what Dr. Carolyn Green called "a look at something that you had never gotten a look at before—the inside of the brain."

The first CT or CAT (computerized axial tomography) imager was introduced in 1972 in the United Kingdom. The CAT scan is an X-ray procedure aided by a computer that produces a three-dimensional view of a part of the body. Dr. Green says that CAT scanning was an important new tool for doctors, especially for patients with problems located in the head. The procedure allowed the early diagnosis of bleeding in the head caused by auto accidents and was a major tool used in caring for premature babies born with brain problems.

Other diagnostic techniques developed with new wonder machines in the 1970s were MRI (magnetic resonance imaging) scanning and PET (positron-emission tomography) scanning.

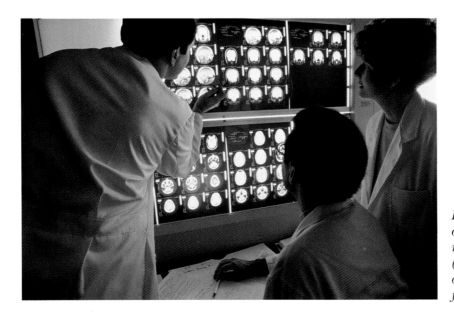

Doctors confer over a series of magnetic resonance images (MRIs) of the head of a person suffering from a brain tumor.

An MRI scan causes what might be described as an atomic broadcast. The hydrogen atoms of the body are caused to release energy. That energy is detected as tiny radio signals, which are then sent to a computer and made into a picture. An MRI gives a more detailed picture of the soft tissues of the body than does a CAT scan.

PET scanning, a technique developed from CAT scanning, allows scientists to actually measure the chemical activity of the brain. Useful for studying such conditions as Alzheimer's disease, strokes, and epilepsy, PET scans can even measure how much brain energy people use when taking tests!

AIDS

Although AIDS (acquired immunodeficiency syndrome) was not officially recognized as a disease until 1981, the first victims began to be seen by doctors in the 1970s. These doctors had no experience in treating a mysterious disease that destroyed the immune system. (The immune system is what allows the body to fight off viruses and other disease-causing organisms.)

Also in the 1970s, the research work was done that allowed scientists to recognize what type of virus causes AIDS. The AIDS virus is a retrovirus. Retroviruses are a special group of viruses. Some retroviruses were known to cause cancer in animals. But it wasn't until the 1970s that Dr. Robert Gallo and his colleagues were able to discover the first human retrovirus. He presented his discovery at scientific meetings in 1979. Dr. Gallo's work with human retroviruses laid the groundwork for later work with AIDS and the development of the AIDS blood test. In his book *Virus Hunting: AIDS, Cancer, and the Human Retrovirus: A Story of Scientific Discovery*, Dr. Gallo wrote that he hopes that his work, done in the 1970s and later, "will contribute to clinical advances that will allow us to treat AIDS patients . . . to develop vaccines for the once-mysterious family of viruses called human retroviruses."

3
EARTH SCIENCES

Earth sciences are those branches of science that study the physical planet, earth, including the water of the earth and the air around the earth. The branches of earth science include geology, hydrology, and meteorology. Many other kinds of science are used in the earth sciences, such as mathematics, physics, chemistry, and even biology. An example of one achievement of the seventies that involved both earth science (in this case, oceanography, a branch of hydrology) and biology were the discoveries made by the research submarine *Alvin*, which are discussed in chapter 2.

Some of the most important advances in the earth sciences in the seventies were in meteorology. Meteorology includes something that we read about in the newspaper every day or watch anxiously on television—especially if we have plans for a picnic or a big ball game. Meteorology, the study of the atmosphere, includes forecasting the weather. During the decade of the seventies, several scientific advances made weather forecasting more accurate—and more interesting to watch on television. It might still rain on our ball game or picnic in the 1990s, but we're more likely to know in advance due to these developments from the 1970s.

Cal Sisto, a meteorologist who broadcasts the weather on a television station in Paducah, Kentucky, sums up the major advances of the seventies in weather forecasting as the result of three things: the first use of Doppler radar, improved satellites, and dramatic developments in computer technology.

SEEING TORNADOES IN TIME

Traditional radar involves a radio system that uses ultrahigh frequency radio waves that bounce off raindrops, snowflakes, and hail present in a cloud system. These radio waves echo back to a radar receiver. By analyzing the radar transmissions, meteorologists can determine the location and severity of rain or snow as it begins to fall. But as useful as this radar is in predicting local weather, it is not very valuable in predicting severe storms such as tornadoes. The high winds from these storms can only be guessed at from a traditional radar picture, and only if the tornado's place in that picture is not lost in the images created by the surrounding rain. That means most tornadoes are not seen by traditional radar in time to give people adequate warning.

But Doppler radar is an important factor in what has been called Nowcasting, a method of processing weather information in a very short time. Named after Christian Doppler, a scientist who lived in the 1800s and discovered what is known as the Doppler effect, Doppler radar is able to see motion in the air, even when snow or rain is not present. The Doppler effect shows that there are changes in frequency when the source of a vibration moves closer to or farther away from the observer. Doppler radar can use existing particles, such as dust and sea salt, in the air to see what is happening inside a cloud system. When the frequency increases, the particles are moving toward the radar site; when the frequency decreases, the particles are moving away from the radar site.

By measuring the speed of particles that are being carried in a storm's winds and the direction of the winds, Doppler radar can determine the wind speeds in a tornado. Meteorologists may be able to recognize the characteristic wind patterns of a tornado in time to warn people before it touches down.

Doppler radar has been used since the 1970s at the U.S. National Severe Storm Laboratory in Norman, Oklahoma, and now is used in other locations throughout the country.

ONE-TENTH OF THE WAY TO THE MOON

On May 14, 1974, the National Oceanic and Atmospheric Administration (NOAA) launched its first geosynchronous, or geostationary, weather satellite. Meteorologist Cal Sisto points out that these types of satellites are approximately 23,000 miles (37,000 kilometers) out in space, almost one-tenth of the way to the moon. Geosynchronous satellites rotate around earth in the same direction as the earth's spin. In this sense, they remain stationary, or in the same place, above a certain place on the earth's surface.

Geosynchronous satellites allow meteorologists to constantly watch one spot on the earth, for instance the Atlantic or Pacific Ocean, for intense storms. An example of their value is the first "hurricane hunter"—a Geostationary Operational Environmental Satellite that was launched into orbit in 1975 to allow the early and close tracking of hurricanes.

Other satellites used in weather forecasting include polar-orbiting satellites, which orbit the Poles and are much closer to the ground, at 460 to 800 miles (740 to 1,290 kilometers) above the earth, and provide more details than the geostationary satellites.

By 1978, the National Weather Service states, the "success of weather satellites caused the elimination of the last U.S. weather observation ship" and "access to satellite data by national centers advanced hurricane, marine, and coastal storm forecasts."

Technicians working on the Meteosat 6, *a French geosynchronous weather satellite*

From Markers to Computer Graphics

Cal Sisto describes the impact of advances in computer technology on weather forecasting in the 1970s as both increasing the ability to forecast weather more quickly and making it more interesting for television viewers to watch.

He says, "Computers were constantly getting more powerful—more capable of doing more calculations in a shorter time, so that they could help accurately figure out what was going to happen in the weather next. We could put more [data] in and we could get more out in shorter time. If we don't get the weather forecast out quickly, there's no sense getting it out at all."

He gives a funny example of the importance of the speed that computers give to weather forecasting: "If you put enough people in a room with a pencil and paper, they could figure the weather out. The problem is that they could figure out tomorrow's forecast in about two weeks."

What about watching the weather? Sisto says, "If I put an old-fashioned weather forecast on, the viewers would fall asleep." He remembers that in

---

MEET CAL SISTO, METEOROLOGIST

Cal Sisto admits that a lot of his interest in the weather began when he was a boy growing up in New Jersey and he "started looking for snow, hoping for days off from school."

He says, though, "Science always interested me. I was born with that." He explains that astronomy was his first love and that when he was in early high school, "The space program captured the nation's imagination. . . . This was very big stuff. But as that [the space program] started to wane, and I started being practical about things, my interest in space waned and at the same time, I was getting more interested in weather."

As he was watching the weather reports for the snow that would mean a day off from school, Cal Sisto says, "I began trying to understand what makes the weather happen, and then I started keeping my own weather records, studying weather instruments, and coming up with my own forecasts. By my sophomore and junior years in high school, I was very much on the track to becoming a meteorologist." He then went on to college, where he, of course, majored in meteorology.

He decided to go into the broadcasting end of being a meteorologist because, "I wanted to communicate to the average person how things work. I wanted to be able to reach the most people possible."

For students who want to be meteorologists, Sisto urges, "Take as many of the math and physical science courses in school as you can get. I am also very strong on emphasizing communications skills—both speaking and writing—for any field."

much of the seventies, weather broadcasts were still done with large maps mounted on the television studio walls. The maps were covered with Plexiglas, and meteorologists used large markers to show weather conditions. The maps could be wiped clean before the next broadcast. But, he says, "The technology to do computer graphics was being developed in the seventies, due to new and better satellite images and the development of smaller but more powerful computers." He thinks that the colors and motion available with computer graphics help make the weather more understandable for television weather watchers.

4

ENVIRONMENTAL SCIENCE

The decade of the 1970s was an extremely important decade in environmental science. Environmental science is simply the study of the environment and the effect people have on it. Environmental science includes scientists working in many fields, such as biology, chemistry, and geology.

All forms of life affect one another. Humans cannot live independently of the earth's other species of plants and animals. Nor can we live well if we destroy the environment—including the air, soil, and water, plus the living things that depend on them. That is why environmental science is so important. We must study how we and our technology are affecting the environment and how we and our technology can cause the least damage. We must also correct damage caused in the past. The English biologist Charles Darwin, who lived from 1809 to 1882, noted the dependence of life-forms upon one another when he studied "a tangled bank, clothed with plants of many kinds, with birds singing on the bushes, with various insects flitting about, and with worms crawling through the damp earth . . . these elaborately constructed forms, so different from each other, and so dependent upon each other in so complex a manner." Perhaps if Darwin had been alive in the 1970s, he would have joined in the first Earth Day!

Environmental activism began in the sixties. The publication of Rachel Carson's book *Silent Spring* in the early part of the decade made both the public and the scientific community aware of how chemicals were affecting animals, humans, and the environment in general. The decade of the seventies was marked by an increase in public involvement in environmental issues and by the passage of several important laws concerned with the environment.

EARTH DAY AND BEYOND

On April 22, 1970, approximately twenty million Americans participated in the first Earth Day. It was called "the biggest demonstration in the history of the nation" and was intended both to help the earth and to make people aware of dangers to the environment from a variety of sources. In celebration of Earth Day, people picked up litter and planted trees. High-school kids rode horses down an expressway, showing an alternative to pollution-causing cars. To protest pollution, a Dead Orange parade was held in Miami, Florida, the home of the Orange Bowl parade, and in New York City, people held up dead fish to symbolize their polluted Hudson River and shouted, "You're next, people."

Did Earth Day make a difference? Philip Shabecoff, the author of *A Fierce Green Fire: The American Environmental Movement*, thinks so. He said in his book, "The millions of Earth Day demonstrators touched off a great burst of activism that profoundly affected the nation's laws, its economy, its corporations, its farms, its politics, science, education, religion, and journalism, created new institutions, and, in time, changed the physical world itself by reducing pollution, and preserving open space and other resources."

Earth Day celebrants inspect newly planted flowers in New York City's Union Square Park on April 22, 1970.

Dr. Philip Handler, who was the president of the National Academy of Sciences in 1970, expressed his worry that some of the people who participated in Earth Day were *blaming* science and technology for pollution. He explained that the best weapon against pollution was the data obtained by scientists. But Dr. Handler felt that the environmental movement, symbolized by Earth Day, was extremely important because, without a widespread feeling that people needed to solve environmental problems, there would not have been money and support available to the scientists who were studying various aspects of the environment.

On the twentieth anniversary of Earth Day, April 22, 1990, more than 200 million people from countries around the world again expressed their continuing concern for the earth and its creatures.

PROTECTING THE ENVIRONMENT, BY LAW

A reflection of the rising concern about how human-caused pollution was affecting the environment was seen in the passage of new laws and the creation of new government agencies in the United States. The National Environmental Policy Act and the Clean Air Act were both passed in 1970. The Occupational Safety and Health Administration (OSHA) was established that same year, as an agency to monitor workplaces, making sure that workers were not exposed to poisonous chemicals and other unhealthy materials, such as asbestos. The Environmental Protection Agency (EPA) was also created in 1970 and was responsible for controlling pollution going into the environment throughout the United States.

Other countries were also becoming aware of the dangers of pollution, the destruction of the habitats of animals and plants, and overpopulation. In 1972, the United Nations held a Conference on the Human Environment and created the United Nations Environmental Program (UNEP). UNEP monitors world pollution and other problems, such as the trade in endangered species.

During the seventies, there was increased awareness of the necessity to save not only the earth itself but our fellow creatures as well. The Marine Mammals Protection Act was passed in 1972, and in 1973, the Endangered Species Act became law. One of the most important events benefiting endangered animals was the banning of DDT, a pesticide used on crops, in the

The bald eagle has made a dramatic comeback since the 1970s.

United States in 1972. (DDT is still used in some countries.) The use of DDT made the eggshells of some birds so thin that their young couldn't develop and hatch properly. Birds such as bald eagles, peregrine falcons, and brown pelicans nearly became extinct. In 1972, before the Endangered Species Act and the banning of DDT, there were fewer than 1,000 bald eagles in the United States. It is encouraging to note that in 1994, there were 8,000 bald eagles alive in the country.

THE LESSON OF LOVE CANAL

One of the most dramatic examples both of the danger to the environment from chemical pollution and of the power of ordinary citizens was demonstrated in the Love Canal area of Niagara Falls, New York, during the period from 1974 to 1978. Citizens there discovered that many residents of Love Canal were developing unexplained illnesses. These illnesses were eventually determined to be caused by chemicals buried underground. Banding together, the citizens of Love Canal brought attention to the company that had buried the dangerous chemicals and eventually received money from the federal government to move away from the area. The company responsible for the pollution had to pay heavy fines and prevent the spreading of the contamination that it had caused.

New Dangers Discovered

Even while the government, scientists, and ordinary citizens were working to solve known environmental problems during the seventies, scientists were also discovering new dangers to the environment.

William H. Brock, the author of *The Norton History of Chemistry*, listed 1972 as the year when scientists identified acid rain. Acid rain is the common name for all acid precipitation, including acidic rain, snow, and fog that are formed when sulfur dioxide and nitrogen oxides are released into the air. These substances are created through the burning of coal and oil and combine with moisture in the air. Acid rain can affect the chemical balance in lakes, rivers, and streams, causing the death of fish and other animals. It can kill trees, sometimes hundreds of miles away from the source of the original pollution. The passage of the Clean Air Act in the United States in 1970 and a number of European agreements beginning in 1979 have helped to reduce acid rain-causing emissions, but acid rain continues to be an environmental concern.

Fir trees in North Carolina clearly show the damage caused by acid rain.

WHAT IS HAPPENING TO THE OZONE?

The ozone layer is part of the stratosphere (the second layer of the atmosphere) and helps protect the earth and its inhabitants from the sun's ultraviolet rays. Changes in the ozone layer could affect crops and weather and could expose people and other species to dangerous ultraviolet radiation.

By the early seventies, scientists were beginning to be concerned about changes in the ozone layer. Scientists warned that nitrogen oxides emitted in the exhaust gases of certain aircraft could affect the ozone layer.

In 1974, chemists F. Sherwood Rowland and Mario Molina performed

---

TECHNOLOGY CAN HELP THE EARTH

Though technology, the process by which people make tools and machines that change and control their environment, can harm the environment, it can help, too:

- When asked about the most important scientific and technological advances of the seventies, Caroline Herzenberg (see interview, chapter 6) says, "Among the major scientific and technical achievements of the 1970s, I would include . . . the development of the supercomputer." Supercomputers can process data faster than other computers and are used in many kinds of science, including weather forecasting, astronomy, medical research, physics, and even environmental science.

- Supercomputers helped scientists in the 1970s develop Global Circulation Models (GCMs). These models simulate conditions, such as increased carbon dioxide emissions produced by burning coal or other fossil fuels. These emissions can cause the earth to warm because heat is trapped by the extra carbon dioxide in the atmosphere. This is called the greenhouse effect. With these models, scientists can look into the future— and hope to change the future of an overheated earth by making changes in how people live now.

- In 1975, French scientists developed a white powder called polynorbornene, a product they planned to use in the manufacture of rubber. It was found that polynorbornene completely absorbs petroleum but does not hurt plants or animals. This product has been used with great success to help clean up oil spills. Oil spills kill many plants and animals, and cleaning them up quickly is an important part of protecting the environment.

An artist's concept of the greenhouse effect

experiments showing that the sunlight in the upper atmosphere could break apart chlorofluorocarbons (CFCs), manufactured molecules that were used in such things as aerosol cans, refrigerators, and air conditioners. The chlorine atoms released when the CFC molecules break apart destroy millions of ozone molecules. The scientists estimated that CFCs could destroy up to 30 percent of the ozone layer by the year 2050. The United States banned the use of CFCs in aerosol cans in 1978. Work is still continuing to find safe substitutes for CFCs in other items. This is important work because during the 1980s, some scientists reported that twice as much ozone was lost over the United States as was predicted. In 1991, the National Aeronautics and Space Administration (NASA) reported that a satellite passing over Antarctica had measured the lowest level yet reported of ozone in the stratosphere.

5

MATHEMATICS

Mathematics, the science of numbers, can be called the language used by other sciences, a language used from archaeology to zoology. An excellent example of how mathematics can help scientists analyze living creatures and can even help create magical monsters and mountains was introduced in 1975.

THE GEOMETRY OF NATURE

In 1975, mathematician Benoit Mandelbrot published his first book of fractals, illustrated with computer images created by physicist Richard Voss.

The word *fractals* comes from a Latin word that means "broken" or "fragmented." Dr. Mandelbrot discovered that nature's irregular shapes, shapes that cannot be measured by lines, planes, and spheres, do have a regular pattern within themselves. That pattern can be studied mathematically. Dr. Mandelbrot found that many natural structures repeat their own pattern over and over, showing the same detailed pattern at a high magnification as at a low magnification. For example, look at a tree and notice its overall structure. Now, look at a branch on that tree. The branch looks like a smaller version of the tree. Now, look at a twig. The twig looks like a still smaller version of the branch. This repeating shape is a fractal. A fractal dimension can be created for the tree's repeating pattern. This is a number that will express the complex fractal form that you have seen in the tree.

The structure of many natural systems, including coastlines, snowflakes, broccoli spears, and even the arteries in a human heart can be studied with fractals. Analyzing natural shapes with fractals could help a doctor study disease in the small arteries of the heart. Fractals have been used to analyze whole swamps. Aerial photographs of the Okefenokee Swamp in Georgia

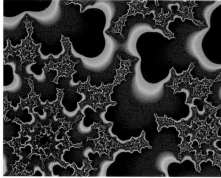

Dr. Benoit Mandelbrot, a pioneer in the study of fractals

have shown that some cypress trees have a fractal dimension. A change in the fractal dimension of these trees could be an early warning that pollution and acid rain could be changing the swamp.

Fractals also allow computers to repeat a fractal shape to create realistic-looking landscapes—and fantastic ones as well. Such computer-generated landscapes can be used as movie sets.

Fractals show that mathematics can help create art and can help us appreciate the beauty of the natural world. Dr. Mandelbrot has compared his discovery to that of introducing the world to beautiful music. He was quoted in *Smithsonian* magazine in December 1983 as saying, "Imagine 100 years ago that singing was outlawed and a great science of analyzing [musical] scores arose. Now think that 100 years later someone looked at these scores and found that they were really much more beautiful and accessible when sung. Beautiful opera scores were appreciated by only a few but beautiful music was appreciated by everyone. I have done that for branches of mathematics."

6

PHYSICS

A great twentieth-century physicist, Niels Bohr, once said, "Physics concerns what we can say about Nature." Physics involves the study of the most basic parts of matter and energy and how they interact to make things work. This interaction of matter and energy affects everything in nature—from our own bodies to the universe as a whole. There are many branches of physics, and in the decade of the seventies, there were important accomplishments and discoveries in several of them.

Particle physics is the study of the most fundamental, or basic, particles that make up matter. This field of study generally involves what is called the quantum theory or quantum mechanics. Cosmology is the study of the universe as a whole, including how it came to be, how it has evolved, or developed, and what its final fate will be. Cosmology often involves work by both physicists and astronomers. Though the specialties within physics can be separated, discoveries in one field often affect another. What we know about fundamental particles affects what we believe about time and space in the universe as a whole, and vice versa.

There were many physics discoveries made in the seventies, from new discoveries about quarks to new information about black holes in space, yet as physicist Heinz R. Pagels said in his book *The Cosmic Code*, "Until the final chapter of physics is written we may be in for lots of surprises."

THE QUARK SHOP: STRAWBERRY, CHOCOLATE, OR VANILLA?

Phillip F. Schewe of the American Institute of Physics says that one of the most important advances in physics in the 1970s was "the development of a standard model concerning the interactions of elementary particles. The apparent discovery in 1994 of the top quark was just the capstone of a long march of experimental and theoretical discoveries, many in the 1970s. The top quark is now believed to be the sixth and final member of a family of truly elementary particles called quarks. They and another family of 6 particles, called leptons, are the constituents of all other, more complicated, objects, such as protons, atoms, and bulk matter."

Quarks therefore are, as far as scientists presently know, fundamental particles of matter. They cannot be divided any further. Quarks make up the neutrons and protons in the nucleus, or central part, of an atom. They were named by scientist Murray Gell-Mann in 1963, after a line in a famous book called *Finnegans Wake* by James Joyce. The word *quark* actually is a German word for a curd of cheese. Until 1974, scientists only knew about three quarks that could combine in different ways to form another unit of matter called the hadron. At one time, physicists named the three quarks chocolate, strawberry, and vanilla. Eventually they changed these names to up, down, and strange, but scientists still refer to quark flavors.

A fourth flavor of quark was discovered in 1974. It was called the charmed quark. This discovery was made possible by advances in the technology of machines called high-energy accelerators. Accelerators probe matter by causing collisions that break the matter into new forms. They might be called matter microscopes.

In 1977, a fifth flavor of quark was discovered. It was called the bottom quark.

Murray Gell-Mann (left) *is shown here with Richard Feynman. Both of these men made vital contributions to the study of physics.*

OTHER ELEMENTARY PARTICLES

Remember that another kind of basic particle was also mentioned by Phillip Schewe: the leptons. Leptons include particles such as electrons, which surround the nucleus of the atom. As early as the 1930s, scientists thought they knew about all of the existing leptons: the electron, the muon, and the neutrino. But in 1977, a new lepton, the tau, was discovered. The tau could be called a very fat electron, as it is like an electron but with a mass about 3,500 times greater.

In 1979, scientists in Hamburg, Germany, observed another class of particles, gluons. Gluons carry the force that causes quarks and other particles to stick together. In *The Cosmic Code*, Dr. Pagels said, "gluons are the glue that holds the world together. Quarks, leptons, and gluons and their organization are all there is in the universe—the ultimate material, the final stuff from which all the complexity of existence emerges."

Phillip Schewe says, "It has taken until this year (1994) to find a 6th quark, the 'top.' Meanwhile theorists in the 1970s worked out the details of how these particles would interact with each other." The establishment of the theory of how the elementary particles interact was one of the great accomplishments of the decade of the seventies.

THE GRAND UNIFIED THEORY: IS IT ALL THE SAME?

There are four forces in nature: the gravitational force, the electromagnetic force, the weak nuclear force, and the strong nuclear force. These forces affect how everything works. But many scientists believe that all of the forces are actually part of one superforce that shows up in different ways. They also predict that particles such as quarks and electrons may turn out to be almost the same thing. A theory that explains this superforce would be a unified theory, sometimes called the grand unified theory, or GUT. It has also been called a theory of everything. Progress was made toward a theory of everything in 1967 when scientists showed the unification of two of the forces, the electromagnetic and the weak nuclear forces. Then, in the seventies, GUT theories were developed that showed that three of the forces, the strong, weak, and electromagnetic forces, could all be different views of one force. These theories, though, did not include gravity.

Another theory, the superstring theory, developed by Michael Green of London University and John Schwarz of the California Institute of Technology, actually proposes that things may not be made up of particles after all, but of loops of string. The superstring theory appears to be able to include gravity as part of one superforce. First considered in the seventies but disregarded until it was later revived and considered a more important theory in the eighties, the superstring theory has been described as a twenty-first-century theory that has been accidentally dropped into the twentieth century. It could be the answer to the theory of everything. Still, one scientist has pointed out that it could take 300 years to fully prove by experimental tests the superstring theory, or any theory of everything.

THE INCOMPARABLE STEPHEN HAWKING

One of the most interesting scientists working in the field of cosmology in the 1970s and since is the British physicist Stephen Hawking. Based on statements in a film about Dr. Hawking and his theories, *A Brief History of Time*, perhaps Stephen Hawking's family could have predicted his future as a physicist interested in the universe. When his mother was in Oxford, England, awaiting Stephen's birth, she went to a store and bought an astronomical atlas. Stephen's aunt said that buying the atlas was a prophetic thing to do.

As Stephen was growing up, his family often read books at the dinner table. His mother has described other family evenings when the family would lie on the grass, using a telescope to see "the wonder of the stars." She remembers that Stephen was especially enchanted by the stars "and further than the stars."

But not all of Stephen's teachers and friends might have predicted his future as an important scientist. One classmate recalls how he and another friend bet a bag of candy over whether or not Stephen would be a success. Stephen's mother remembers one year in school when he was third from the bottom in his class. She asked him if he had to be as far down as that. He told her that a lot of the students hadn't done much better. His mother remembers that he was "quite unconcerned."

Perhaps Stephen was not concerned because he realized that he had a special gift for math and physics. A college classmate recalls when he,

Stephen, and some other friends had to read a chapter in a book called *Electricity of Magnetism* and answer thirteen very difficult questions. Stephen's friend worked for a week and was able to finish one and a half questions, of which he was very proud. At the end of the week, Stephen had not even started the questions. He sat down for three hours and worked. His friend asked how many he had completed. "Well," Stephen said, "I've only had time to do the first ten."

Stephen's friend recalls realizing then, "It's not just that we weren't on the same street, we weren't even on the same planet."

Still, Stephen Hawking admits that he didn't work very hard while in college at Oxford. He says that he was very bored, that "there had not seemed to be anything worth doing."

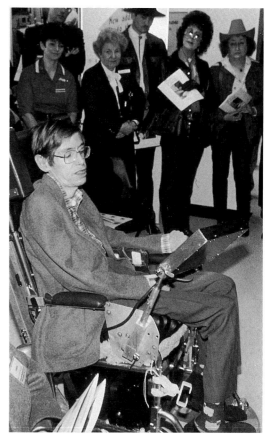

Stephen Hawking, a brilliant physicist, worked to develop a quantum theory of gravity.

But then, when he was twenty-one, he was diagnosed with a terrible illness called amyotrophic lateral sclerosis, or Lou Gehrig's disease. He was told that his body would eventually deteriorate to the point that he would have the body of a cabbage. His mind would still be functioning, but he would have no way to communicate with the rest of the world. He was told that he had only two and one-half years to live.

At this time, Stephen had a dream in which he was about to be executed. When he woke up, he knew that there were many "worthwhile things that I could do." He wanted to live and be able to do these things.

Though Stephen Hawking's disease has not been cured, his doctors were wrong. He has been alive (in 1995) for more than fifty years and can communicate with the world through the use of a special computer. And, in the seventies, Stephen Hawking developed a theory that some scientists said changed *everything*.

HAWKING'S BRILLIANT THEORY

In order to understand what Stephen Hawking discovered, it is first important to backtrack a bit and discuss the two theories of physics developed in the twentieth century. In his book *A Brief History of Time*, Stephen Hawking wrote, "Today scientists describe the universe in terms of two basic partial theories—the general theory of relativity and quantum mechanics. They are the great intellectual achievements of the first half of this century." The general theory of relativity describes how gravity works on the universe as a whole, such as how it affects stars, planets, and galaxies. Quantum mechanics describes how things on a very small scale—atoms and even smaller particles—work and are affected by forces. Stephen Hawking said, "Unfortunately, however, these two theories are known to be inconsistent with each other—they cannot both be correct. One of the major endeavors in physics today . . . is the search for a new theory that will incorporate them both—a quantum theory of gravity."

Remember that in the discussion about the theory of everything, gravity was not part of the unified theory. Gravitational force must be accounted for in a truly complete unified theory. In the seventies, Stephen Hawking took the first step toward developing a quantum theory of gravity.

In the general theory of relativity, developed by Albert Einstein in 1915, there is a prediction of a single definite path within space and time for each particle. But in quantum mechanics, a theory developed in the 1920s, there is an element of uncertainty. This might be compared to playing a game with dice. There are several ways that the dice can fall, and you cannot be sure of the way. Albert Einstein did not accept this element of chance. He said, "God does not play dice." But does He? Stephen Hawking has said that "not only does God play dice, He sometimes throws them where they cannot be seen."

Dr. Hawking's theory concerns black holes. A black hole is thought to be a region of space that has such powerful gravity that anything that comes too close to it, even light, will be pulled in and can never escape. A black hole could be compared to a superpowerful vacuum cleaner. The general theory of relativity explains some things about black holes, but the quantum theory is needed to explain black holes more fully.

Quantum mechanics says that in space there are pairs of matter particles. One of the pair is actually an antiparticle. One particle has positive energy and one has negative. These particles are constantly getting rid of each other. They are keeping things in balance by canceling each other out.

But what if the particles were separated? In her book *Stephen Hawking: Quest for a Theory of Everything*, Kitty Ferguson explained Dr. Hawking's 1973 theory this way: "The way he pictures it, a pair of virtual particles appears. Before the pair meet again and annihilate [destroy each other], the one with negative energy crosses the event horizon into the black hole." Because of a change in the property of the particles due to the gravitational field at the event horizon (the boundary of the black hole), the particles "are no longer obliged to find one another and annihilate. . . . The particle with positive energy might fall into the black hole, too, of course, but it doesn't have to. It's free of the partnership. It can escape. To an observer at a distance it appears to come out of the black hole. In fact, it comes from just outside. Meanwhile, its partner has carried negative energy into the black hole."

This radiation (radiation is the movement of energy, in this case the positive energy) that is produced by the black hole is called Hawking radiation. Hawking's theory shows that the black hole, which is receiving the negative energy, might get smaller until it finally disappears completely. The negative energy actually causes the energy present inside the black hole to become less and less. But why would this make the black hole disappear? Einstein's famous equation $E = mc^2$ means

Stephen Hawking combined Einstein's general theory of relativity with quantum mechanics and revolutionized the field of physics.

that the energy (E) equals the mass (m) times the speed of light (c) squared. The speed of light doesn't change, so what can change is the energy and the mass. So in order to keep things equal if the energy grows less in the black hole, the mass also decreases. The decrease in mass can allow the black hole to get smaller and smaller.

Unless we have a mind like Stephen Hawking's, this can all be difficult to understand and remember! But one thing to remember is that, as Hawking wrote in *A Brief History of Time*, "The idea of radiation from black holes was the first example of a prediction that depended in an essential way on example of a spectrum occurs when a beam of light passes through a prism and shows a group of colors. The spectra that Dr. Herzenberg measured were the tiny differences in the energy of the gamma rays that were absorbed by the different samples.) My work with this technique was especially worthwhile . . . because it permitted entirely nondestructive analysis of valuable and irreplaceable samples.

Author: How did you feel when you held the materials from the moon in your hands? Can you describe how the rocks and soil looked and felt?

Dr. Herzenberg: I worked with small pieces of moon rock the size of pebbles and also with samples of the fines (moondust). It was tremendously exciting to actually hold pieces of the moon in my hands.

Author: Looking back on your work done in the seventies, why do you feel it is especially important today?

Dr. Herzenberg: In thinking about past work, I find it helpful to recall the . . . remarks ascribed to Isaac Newton (an important seventeenth-century physicist and mathematician) . . . that he was able to achieve his immense accomplishments because he had the benefit of the achievements of his scientific predecessors and was "standing on the shoulders of giants." This is true of all of us in our more limited ways, and our minor accomplishments in turn provide parts of the foundation on which subsequent science is developed. The first scientists who worked on the *Apollo* program had the great privilege of scoping out new aspects of lunar science and laid the groundwork for much of the research in lunar science that has been conducted subsequently.

Author: What do you suggest students who are interested in physics do to work toward physics as a future career?

Dr. Herzenberg: Develop and value your intuition. Get a good background in mathematics. Develop computer skills. Do as much hands-on science as you can. Go on industrial and laboratory tours and field trips whenever you can. Don't be discouraged from having a lot of fun doing science!

both the great theories of this century, general relativity and quantum mechanics."

Stephen Hawking's theory, developed in the seventies, may have put scientists on their way toward a complete theory of everything. But Stephen Hawking hoped that not just scientists but *everyone* would be able to understand this theory. He wrote, "If we do discover a complete theory, it should in time be understandable in broad principle by everyone, not just a few scientists. Then we shall all . . . be able to take part in the discussion of the question of why it is that we and the universe exist. If we find the answer to that, it would be the ultimate triumph of human reason—for then we would know the mind of God."

How Discoveries in Physics Affect Us Every Day

Much of the work discussed in this section was in theoretical physics, theories about how matter and the forces that act upon it work. In *A Brief History of Time*, Stephen Hawking explained why he works in theoretical physics by saying, "The search for the ultimate theory of the universe seems difficult to justify on practical grounds. The discovery of a complete unified theory . . . may not even affect our life-style. But ever since the dawn of civilization, people have not been content to see events as unconnected and inexplicable. . . . Humanity's deepest desire for knowledge is justification enough for our continuing quest."

While Stephen Hawking made an important point, it is also important to know that advances in many fields of physics *have* made changes in our everyday lives. Such things as electric lights, jet planes, television, and computers would have been impossible without a knowledge of physics. Two advances of the 1970s mentioned by Phillip Schewe of the American Institute of Physics illustrate this point.

He lists the first of these advances as the development of multilayered semiconductor devices. He explains that "the ability to conduct electricity is important from the standpoint of practical electronic devices. Metals are good conductors. Ceramics are poor conductors; in fact, they are used as insulators. Semiconductor materials, such as silicon, conduct poorly unless they are tweaked by the application of a slight voltage. The important feature here is that their conducting state can be altered very quickly, a great advantage in the storage and processing of information. In the 1970s, great progress was made in manipulating the properties of certain semiconductor layer cakes . . . consisting of very different materials. Such structures could be tailored to produce different electronic effects. Physics research in this area was immediately taken up by, and was promoted by, the ongoing revolution in computer design in the 1970s."

The other area that might change our lives someday, by providing the world with cheap, clean energy, was "progress toward the establishment of controlled nuclear fusion." Nuclear fusion happens when two atomic nuclei

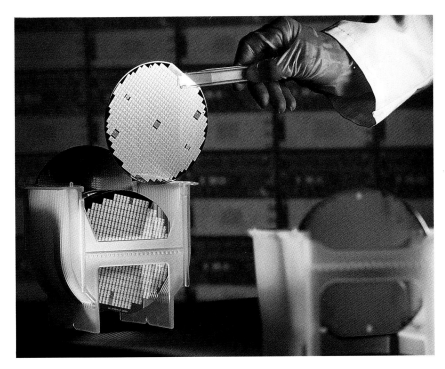

Semiconductor wafers are shown here being tested in a quality control lab.

collide and fuse at high temperatures. When this happens, the bonds holding the neutrons and protons together inside the nuclei are broken and a new, larger nucleus is formed. Energy is released by this reaction in the form of particles that speed out of the colliding nuclei. If these particles are used to hit a solid target, heat will result, which could be used to change water into steam, which can then be used to drive engines that generate electricity. The energy produced from the fusion of a form of hydrogen, deuterium, found in seawater, gives an example of the potential uses of fusion. If fusion could be created using just the top 10 feet (3 meters) of the oceans, the energy needs of the world could be met for the next fifty million years!

In the seventies, Phillip Schewe says, "Scientists sought to produce sustained reactions, like those at the center of the sun, in which hydrogen atoms, stripped of their electrons, could be forced together with a release of energy. This research continues to this day."

7

ASTRONOMY AND SPACE EXPLORATION

In some ways, after the tremendous accomplishment of putting a man on the moon in 1969, the following decade may seem like something of a letdown in space exploration. However, a number of important discoveries were made in space during the seventies—by those observing the universe from earth, by those who were lucky enough to go into space, and by the machines that humans sent into space to observe for them.

People have probably always watched the skies and studied the celestial, or heavenly, bodies of the universe, including the planets and their satellites, comets, meteors, and stars. More than 4,000 years ago, people in China were recording the motions of celestial bodies. In the seventies, astronomers used new telescopes to view the matter of the universe, as well as satellites and even space probes that could be sent out into the solar system to view the planets. New discoveries were made of things that can be seen—and even of matter that is invisible.

DARK MATTER AND OTHER MATTERS

When astronomer Vera Rubin was a child, she had a north-facing window where she watched the stars and planets. She says, "I had a bed under a window as a child . . . and found it more interesting to watch the stars than to sleep." Her father helped her build a telescope, and Vera was on her way to becoming an astronomer. Caroline Herzenberg, the scientist interviewed in chapter 6, says that "Vera Rubin made several important discoveries during the 1970s. She studied the rotation of galaxies and showed that galaxies rotate more rapidly near their edges than could be accounted for by the gravitational forces from the amount of visible mass contained in the galaxies.

Thus she discovered that there was missing mass that indicated there must be dark matter in the galaxies."

Scientists are not sure what this dark matter really is, but Dr. Rubin's discovery about the motion of outlying stars must mean that there is invisible matter that is affecting how fast they move. Her discovery showed that all of the matter we can see, for example, stars, is really no more than about 10 percent of the total mass that is out there in our galaxy, the Milky Way. As Donald Goldsmith wrote about Vera Rubin's discovery in his book *The Astronomers*, "Rubin's research implies that all the visible matter in the universe forms only a sort of light frosting on the cosmic cake, which consists basically of invisible matter."

ADVANCES IN ASTRONOMY

In 1977, a team of astronomers, including James Elliot, discovered to their surprise that the planet Uranus has a system of rings. While recording Uranus passing in front of a star, the astronomers observed that the star dimmed briefly a number of times before it was shadowed by the actual planet. They figured out that this meant that Uranus had at least nine narrow rings that were shadowing the star before Uranus itself passed across. Later, in 1986, *Voyager 2* (see page 65), showed that Uranus had two additional rings.

The rings are made up of chunks of material the size of boulders. Some scientists think that the rings of Uranus may be made up of parts of a moon that was once torn apart by the effects of the gravity of Uranus. The material that makes up the rings is black—some of the darkest material found in our solar system.

Another surprising discovery in astronomy was made by James Christy in 1978. Christy was trying to measure Pluto's size but noticed that Pluto did not seem to be the right shape. It seemed to be longer in one part than in another. He then realized that Pluto had a moon about 10,563 miles (16,900 kilometers) from it. Pluto is the smallest of the nine planets and the farthest from the sun (though at certain times in its orbit, Pluto is actually closer to the sun than its neighbor planet, Neptune). Because it is generally the planet farthest from the sun, Pluto was named after the Greek and Roman god of the dark underworld of the dead. It is no surprise then that the planet Pluto's

The planet Pluto, discovered in 1930, was found to have a moon in 1978. These two heavenly bodies were first photographed in 1990 by the Hubble Space Telescope.

newly discovered moon was named after Charon, the boatman in Greek mythology who ferried the dead to Pluto's kingdom.

THE FIRST BLACK HOLE?

Black holes are invisible, so how can scientists know where in the universe one exists? In *A Brief History of Time*, Stephen Hawking explained, "Astronomers have observed many systems in which two stars orbit around each other by gravity. They also observe systems in which there is only one visible star that is orbiting around some unseen companion. One cannot . . . conclude that the companion is a black hole: it might merely be a star that is too faint to be seen. However, some of these systems . . . are also strong sources of X rays [a type of radiation]. The best explanation for this phenomenon is that matter has been blown off the surface of the visible star. As it falls toward the unseen companion, it develops a spiral motion (rather like water running out of a bath), and it gets very hot, emitting X rays. . . . For this mechanism to work, the unseen object has to be very small, like . . . a black hole."

In 1971, a special satellite carrying equipment that could pinpoint the exact location of X rays showed that the source of X rays coming from the constellation Cygnus in the northern sky was a massive but invisible object.

Dr. Hawking explained that the mass (the amount of matter that is in an object; a very small object can have a very large mass) of this invisible object is "about six times the mass of the sun." An invisible object with this much mass fits the definition of a black hole. Dr. Hawking concluded, "It seems, therefore, that it must be a black hole."

Scientists named the system of the invisible object and the stars that are orbiting around each other Cygnus X-1. This is believed to be the first discovery of a black hole.

An X-ray image shows the binary star system known as Cygnus X-1.

THE SPACE PROBES

Not only did scientists in the seventies have telescopes and other technology on earth to help them explore the universe, but they also had machines that could travel through our solar system and beyond, returning data and pictures to earth.

The Soviet Union's spacecraft *Luna 16* was the first probe not operated by people to return soil samples from the moon. The craft landed in the area of the moon named the Sea of Fertility on September 20, 1970, and sent out a 35-inch (89-centimeter) arm with a drill on its end. Within a mere seven minutes, a scoop of moon matter was ready to be returned to earth. *Luna 16* provided scientists on earth with 220 pounds (100 kilograms) of moon samples to study.

On November 17, 1970, a Soviet spacecraft, *Luna 17*, landed in the region of the moon called the Sea of Rains. This craft released the first remote-controlled roving vehicle to travel the moon, the *Lunokhod 1*. It had eight wheels and was 3 feet (0.9 meter) high and 4 feet (1.2 meters) long. The *Lunokhod 1* was like a big remote-controlled car that could be driven by a team of five men at Mission Control in Moscow. It carried instruments such as X-ray telescopes that could observe the galaxy and an X-ray soil analyzer that could give scientists information about the moon's soil. The rover also carried two TV cameras that could return pictures to earth. *Lunokhod 1* operated for almost a year and sent 20,000 pictures back to earth. On January 16, 1973, a similar moon vehicle, *Lunokhod 2*, was released on the moon by *Luna 21*. Carrying an extra TV camera, *Lunokhod 2* operated for close to five months and returned 80,000 pictures to earth.

On November 13, 1971, *Mariner 9*, a probe sent by NASA, reached Mars. Orbiting Mars for almost a year, *Mariner 9* mapped most of the surface of Mars and discovered the largest known volcano in the solar system. It was named Olympus Mons. The ancient Greeks considered Mount Olympus to be the home of their powerful gods. A majestic name was needed for this enormous volcano, and Olumpus Mons fit the bill. The volcano was found to be about three times higher than Mount Everest in the Himalaya Mountains on earth. Mount Everest is the highest point on earth and is 29,002 feet (8,700 meters) high. This means that Olympus Mons is about 90,000 feet (27,000 meters) high!

Mariner 10 was launched on November 3, 1973. It flew past Venus in February 1974 and then went on in March 1974 to be the first probe to fly past Mercury, the planet closest to the sun. Flying within 187 miles (300 kilometers) of Mercury, *Mariner* was able to return the first pictures of that planet's surface. *Mariner 10*'s pictures of Mercury revealed a rocky planet with many craters. It appeared that volcanoes had been present some time in Mercury's past. An enormous crater was discovered and named the Caloris Basin. The Caloris Basin is 812 miles (1,300 kilometers) across—approximately equal to the width of 17,864 soccer fields lined up side by side!

On December 3, 1973, *Pioneer 10* (launched on March 3, 1972) became the first probe to fly by Jupiter. *Pioneer 11*, launched on April 5, 1973, reached Jupiter a year later. The *Pioneer* cameras sent back pictures of

Jupiter showing a giant world of clouds. On September 1, 1979, *Pioneer 11* became the first probe to reach Saturn. The pictures *Pioneer 11* returned to earth showed a new moon and a new outer ring.

The twin spacecraft *Pioneer 10* and *Pioneer 11* hold the distinction of being the first probes to leave our solar system and act as our messengers to the stars. In case these craft someday encounter intelligent life, both carry a gold-plated plaque. The plaque shows drawings of a man and a woman standing next to the outline of a spacecraft. These drawings are meant to give other life-forms a glimpse of the creatures that sent such a spacecraft out to travel among the stars.

On December 15, 1970, the Soviet craft *Venera 7* made the first landing on Venus, but it wasn't until October 22, 1975 that *Venera 9* returned the first glimpses of the surface of Venus to earth through its TV camera. The area that was viewed by the cameras on *Venera 9* and later *Venera* craft revealed a landscape that was covered with rocks and stones. *Venera* craft in the eighties, however, did find areas that were not covered with stones.

Although the *Mariner* probes had explored much of Mars while in orbit,

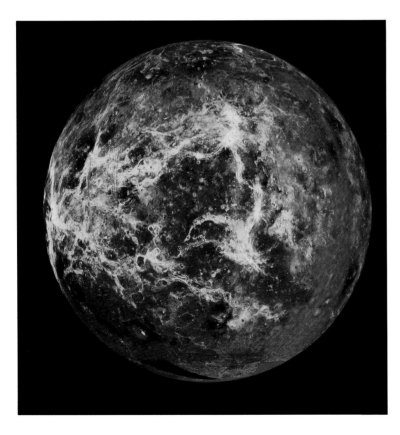

This is a false-color radar map of the western hemisphere of Venus. Color cues were taken from Soviet photographic data gathered during several Venera *missions.*

NASA was not finished with its exploration of Mars in the seventies. It launched two new craft, *Viking 1* and *Viking 2*, in August and September 1975. *Viking 1* landed on the red planet on July 20, 1976. *Viking 2* landed on September 3, 1976. The *Viking*s sent back TV pictures of Mars showing rocky deserts, sand dunes, and rocks with so many holes that they looked like blocks of Swiss cheese. The pictures also revealed pink skies that are due to red dust scattering the light of Mars.

THE *VOYAGERS*

More advanced than the *Pioneer* probes, *Voyagers 1* and *2* were launched in 1977. These probes have sent, and continue to send, information about our solar system.

In the 1960s, scientist Gary Flandro realized that the gravity of one planet could possibly be used to speed up a space probe and sling it toward another planet, a sort of giant slingshot effect. This would allow a probe to reach the otherwise unreachable planets of Jupiter, Saturn, Uranus, and Neptune. In the seventies, these giant planets orbited into positions that put the four planets in a line. This created an opportunity for a probe to use Jupiter's gravity to boost the craft to Saturn. Saturn's gravity could then push the probe to Uranus. Uranus's gravity could then at last push the craft to Neptune. Such a lucky alignment would not take place again for another 176 years! Fortunately, scientists were able to take advantage of this alignment with both the *Pioneer* and *Voyager* probes.

The Voyager *mission patch shows the probe leaving Earth and traveling to Jupiter, Saturn, and beyond.*

A RECORD OF OUR CIVILIZATION

When *Voyagers 1* and *2* left earth in 1977, these space probes each carried a record called "Sounds of Earth." It was hoped that if there are intelligent beings in space, they might find the record and learn about our civilization here on earth.

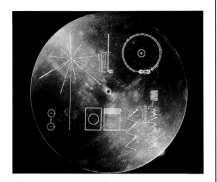

"Sounds of Earth"

The record was the idea of scientist Carl Sagan. It is made of gold-plated copper and is inside a protective aluminum jacket. An advanced civilization could use electronic information on the record to show diagrams, pictures, and text. Some of the things recorded on the "Sounds of Earth" are laughter, heartbeats, whales singing, train whistles, crying, kissing, thunder, wind, music of many kinds (classical, jazz, rock and roll), and hellos in about sixty earth languages. There are 115 photographs and diagrams telling about mathematics, chemistry, geology, biology, and about our technology and society. There are also descriptions of our solar system and our DNA and photographs of earth and human beings from many countries, doing many things.

No one knows if the "Sounds of Earth" record will ever be heard by extraterrestrial beings. Dr. Sagan has described it as a "bottle into the cosmic ocean."

In 1979, *Voyagers 1* and *2* flew close enough to Jupiter to send home much new information with their television cameras and instruments. The *Voyagers* revealed that the planet has a ring around it and that one of Jupiter's moons, Io, had a volcano erupting on its surface. One scientist, Bradford Smith, also gave Io a new name. He said it looked better than a lot of pizzas, and Io has since been nicknamed the pizza moon!

The Last Trip (?) to the Moon and Other *Apollo* Missions

Budget cuts and waning public interest in the space program caused a reduction in what was achieved in the seventies in space exploration as compared to the decade of the sixties. But there were still important flights by people eager to go into space.

Is the number thirteen lucky or unlucky? For the crew of moon mission *Apollo 13*, it could have been considered both. An oxygen tank explosion destroyed the power system and oxygen supply of the command module on *Apollo 13* on April 13, 1970, threatening the lives of astronauts James Lovell,

John Swigert, and Fred Haise. The command module was the part of the spacecraft that the astronauts were supposed to use to return to earth.

The astronauts had only one chance to survive. They decided to use the lunar module as a lifeboat. The lunar module was the part of the spacecraft designed to land on the moon but not made to return to earth. The lunar module still had its oxygen and power supply—enough to last for thirty-eight hours. But the astronauts were at least ninety hours from home! Carrying along the crippled command module, which they would have to have to reenter earth's atmosphere, the astronauts turned all their equipment down as low as possible to save power, and traveled in cold and darkness toward survival. Before reentering the earth's atmosphere, the astronauts transferred back into the crippled command module, which luckily was able to survive reentry and splashed down into the Pacific Ocean on April 17.

Though the *Apollo 13* mission was not able to land on the moon, the fact that its crew was able to survive such an accident was a triumph in itself. Thinking back on the mission twenty-five years later, astronaut Jim Lovell said, "The fact that we triumphed over an almost certain catastrophe does give me a deep sense of satisfaction. Although I didn't land on the moon, the achievement that was accomplished, I thought, was well worthwhile to participate in."

Unfortunately, luck was not with Soviet cosmonauts Georgi Dobrovolsky, Vladislav Volkov, and Viktor Patseyev in 1971. The cosmonauts had spent twenty-four days in *Salyut 1*, the Soviet space station. *Salyut 1*, which was launched into orbit on June 6, 1971, was the first operational space station. During their mission, the cosmonauts had observed the stars, grown crops in a greenhouse, and even hatched frog eggs! Cosmonaut Dobrovolsky had said about *Salyut 1*, "This place is tremendous. There seems to be no end to it!"

Sadly, on their return to earth, the three cosmonauts were found dead. Experts believe that during reentry into the earth's atmosphere, a valve on their spacecraft opened, letting air out of the cabin, killing the men.

The year 1971 also saw two more flights to the moon from the United States.

Apollo 14 was launched on January 31, 1971, with Alan Shepard, Stuart Roosa, and Edgar Mitchell on board. *Apollo 14*'s lunar module landed in a hilly area of the moon, an area covered with rocky matter that scientists think was thrown out when giant meteorites hit the moon in the past. *Apollo 14* returned to earth with 96 pounds (44 kilograms) of samples from the moon.

Apollo 15 was launched on July 26, 1971. Its crew consisted of David Scott, Alfred Worden, and James Irwin. *Apollo 15* also carried a special car, a rover that could move across the moon, carrying astronauts and equipment, such as a television camera. The rover was nicknamed the moon buggy. It cost about $13 million to build!

Astronaut David Scott proved that one of Galileo's theories was right. Galileo was a famous astronomer and physicist who lived from 1564 to 1642. He had said that without the air resistance present on earth, every body, whether heavy or light, would fall at the same rate. David Scott dropped a hammer and a feather at the same time on the airless moon and watched them hit the ground at the same time. "How about that," he said. "Mr. Galileo was correct."

Apollo 16 was launched on April 16, 1972. The astronauts aboard were John W. Young, Thomas K. Mattingly, and Charles M. Duke Jr. The lunar module landed in an area of the moon that scientists believe was produced by volcanoes. This mission returned 170 pounds (77 kilograms) of samples to earth.

Apollo 17 was the last moon flight from the United States—at least so far. Launched on December 7, 1972, its crew included Eugene Cernan, Ronald Evans, and Harrison Schmitt. *Apollo 17* was the first nighttime launch. Harrison Schmitt, a geologist, was especially helpful in locating samples from the moon that would include evidence of volcanoes. *Apollo 17* brought back 243 pounds (110 kilograms) of samples. Eugene Cernan was the last astronaut to walk on the moon. Interviewed by science writer Frank White in his book *The Overview Effect: Space Exploration and Human Evolution*, Eugene Cernan said about sharing his experiences with others, "The native folks in West Africa, for example, seemingly out of touch . . . wanted to know what it [the moon] looked like. . . . They somehow wanted to be there through us. . . . The space program by its very nature . . . brought the world closer. It is truly one of the greatest endeavors in the history of mankind."

On July 15, 1975, two spacecraft were launched as part of a joint space mission uniting two rivals: the United States and the Soviet Union. The

Soviet Union's *Soyuz* craft and the United States' *Apollo* craft both blasted off on the 15th so that they could meet in orbit on July 17. As *Apollo* reached orbit, Donald "Deke" Slayton, who at the age of fifty-one was the oldest man to have flown in space, said that it had been "worth waiting sixteen years for." A special docking module, or unit, was carried by *Apollo*. This module allowed the docking, or joining together in space, of the two craft.

Over the next forty-four hours, while their craft were docked, the crew from the United States, Thomas Stafford, Vance Brand, and Donald Slayton, and that of the Soviet Union, Alexei Leonov and Valeri Kubasov, became friends. They ate together and did joint science experiments.

This space mission was a symbol of the friendship that can be created— even among rivals. This friendship was also something truly worth waiting for.

An artist's concept illustrating an Apollo-*type spacecraft* (top) *about to dock with a Soviet* Soyuz-*type spacecraft. The illustration, created in 1973, looked ahead to the actual* Apollo-Soyuz *mission, which took place in 1975.*

Right: *Deke Slayton is seen in the hatchway leading from the* Apollo *docking module to the* Soyuz *orbital module.*

THE SPACE SHUTTLE, AND A SPACE STATION

At his inauguration in January 1973, President Richard Nixon announced his approval of the Space Transportation System—the space shuttle. This

---

MEET R. MIKE MULLANE, ASTRONAUT

Astronaut R. Mike Mullane often visits schools to tell about how he became an astronaut and about his experiences as a mission specialist astronaut on space shuttle flights. But you don't have to wait for him to come to your school. You can meet him right now!

Mullane was selected by NASA to be an astronaut in 1978. This was the fulfillment of his dream, a dream that he thought might never come true.

In his talks and in his book *Liftoff! An Astronaut's Dream*, Mullane says, "I can still see myself as a small child, dreaming about flying. It was almost as if I was born with that dream." The year that he was eleven, he wanted a telescope more than anything else. Mullane got his wish and spent many hours on Christmas night watching the planets. He says, "I stood for a moment and stared at the dome of the heavens. Venus had set. Saturn and Jupiter and the moon would be up for many more hours. . . . I watched and I wished. . . . I wished I could fly into space."

Mullane remembers when Neil Armstrong became the first person to walk on the moon on July 20, 1969. Mike Mullane wanted badly to be an astronaut, too, but he didn't think that would ever be possible. He had graduated from West Point by this time and knew that because he wore glasses, he could never be a test pilot—and NASA only picked test pilots to become astronauts.

But Mike Mullane continued to work hard. He went back to college to become an aeronautical engineer in the seventies. He says, "If I couldn't be a pilot or an astronaut, I could still help to design and test the planes and rockets that the pilots and astronauts would fly."

It was a good thing that Mullane kept himself involved in aeronautics (the science of flight), because in the seventies, NASA began looking for a new kind of astronaut, called a mission specialist. These astronauts "would do experiments and space walks and release satellites. . . . Mission specialists didn't have to be pilots! They could wear glasses! . . . The dream was back!"

Mike Mullane was selected from over 10,000 applicants to fill one of thirty-five astronaut positions. He entered the space program in 1978 and says that the emphasis at that time was to finish testing and get a space shuttle ready to fly, which happened three years later. He explains that the space shuttle (called the STS by NASA) is important because it is recyclable. "Before the shuttle, all of our rockets, including the moon rockets, were 'throwaway' rockets. . . . But almost all of the STS can be reused, which saves money."

R. Mike Mullane says that the future for space exploration includes building space stations in partnership with other nations. And he says that NASA's "grand plan is to return to the moon and even to send people to Mars." He asks the students who hear his talks or read his book, "Who will be the first human to set foot on the red planet? Could it be you?"

---

new spacecraft was designed to be reusable, which would make it much less expensive than previous spacecraft, which could not be reused. President Nixon said, "The United States should proceed at once with the development of an entirely new type of space transportation system design to help transform the space frontier of the 1970s into familiar territory, easily accessible for human endeavor in the 1980s and 1990s. It will revolutionize transportation into near space [the space shuttles are not meant to fly as far as the moon] by routinizing it. It will take the astronomical costs out of astronautics."

NASA began conducting tests in February of 1977 of the space shuttle *Enterprise*, named after the spaceship in the popular television show *Star Trek*. These tests took place over the Mojave Desert in California, beginning the journey toward a space shuttle, the *Columbia*, that would be launched into space in 1981.

On May 14, 1977, NASA launched its first space station, *Skylab*. *Skylab* was designed to allow astronauts to spend time in space, performing experiments, and to determine the effects of long periods in space. There were three crews that visited *Skylab* during 1977. The first crew stayed in space for twenty-eight days. The last crew stayed in space for eighty-four days! *Skylab* astronauts did medical experiments, such as taking blood samples from each other and checking how well their blood was circulating and their hearts were functioning. They took photographs of the sun and the earth. They even did an experiment, suggested by high-school students, to see how well spiders could spin webs in the zero gravity of space. The spiders, named Anita and Arabella, proved that they could spin webs even in zero G's.

Sources

Booth, Nicholas. *The Encyclopedia of Space*. New York: Mallard Press, 1990.

Goldsmith, Donald. *The Astronomers*. New York: St. Martin's Press, 1991.

Goodall, Jane. *Through a Window: My Thirty Years With the Chimpanzees of Gombe*. Boston: Houghton Mifflin, 1990.

Horner, John R., and James Gorman. *Digging Dinosaurs*. New York: Workman Publishing Company, 1988; New York: Harper and Row, 1990.

Johanson, Donald, and James Shreeve. *Lucy's Child: The Discovery of a Human Ancestor*. New York: William Morrow, 1989.

Kerrod, Robin. *The Journeys of Voyager: NASA Reaches for the Planets*. New York: Mallard Press, 1990.

Lessem, Don. *Dinosaurs Rediscovered*. New York: Simon and Schuster, Touchstone, 1993. (First published as *Kings of Creation*, 1992.)

McDermott, Jeanne. "Geometrical Forms Known as Fractals Find Sense in Chaos." *Smithsonian*, December 1983.

Shabecoff, Philip. *A Fierce Green Fire: The American Environmental Movement*. New York: Hill and Wang, 1993.

Further Reading

Asimov, Isaac. *How Did We Find Out About Atoms.* New York: Walker and Co., 1976.

Averous, Pierre. The Atom. Hauppauge, N.Y.: Barron, 1988.

Chenel, Pascale. Life and Death of Dinosaurs. Hauppauge, N.Y.: Barron, 1987.

Darling, David. *Genetic Engineering: Redrawing the Blueprint of Life.* Morristown, N.J.: Silver Burdett, 1995.

Diagram Group Staff and David Lambert. *The Field Guide to Early Man.* New York: Facts on File, 1988.

Farlow, James O. *On the Tracks of Dinosaurs: A Study of Dinosaur Footprints.* New York: Franklin Watts, 1991.

Ferguson, Kitty. *Stephen Hawking: Quest for a Theory of Everything.* New York: Franklin Watts, 1991; New York: Bantam, 1992.

Greenberg, Keith. *Hurricanes and Tornadoes.* New York: Twenty-First Century Books, 1994.

Gutfreund, Geraldine Marshall. *Vanishing Animal Neighbors.* New York: Franklin Watts, 1993.

Horner, Jack, and Don Lessem. *Digging Up Tyrannosaurus Rex.* New York: Crown, 1992.

Johnson, Rebecca L. *Diving Into Darkness: A Submersible Explores the Sea.* Minneapolis: Lerner, 1989.

McVey, Vicki. *Sierra Club Book of Weatherwisdom.* Boston: Little, Brown, 1991.

Mogil, H. Michael, and Barbara G. Levine. *The Amateur Meteorologist: Explorations and Investigations.* New York: Franklin Watts, 1993.

Mullane, R. Mike. *Liftoff! An Astronaut's Dream.* Parsippany, N.J.: Silver Burdett Press, 1995.

Roberts, Royston M. *Serendipity: Accidental Discoveries in Science.* New York: John Wiley and Sons, 1989.

Shulman, Jeffrey, and Teresa Rogers. *Gaylord Nelson: A Day for the Earth.* New York: Twenty-First Century Books, 1992.

Shorto, Russell. *How to Fly the Space Shuttle.* Santa Fe, N.M.: John Muir, 1992.

Vogt, Gregory. *The Space Shuttle.* Brookfield, Conn.: Millbrook Press, 1991.

_____. *Viking and the Mars Landing.* Brookfield, Conn.: Millbrook Press, 1991.

Wilcox, Frank H. DNA: *The Thread of Life.* Minneapolis: Lerner, 1988.

Index

References to illustrations are listed in *italic, **boldface*** type.

About the Author

Geraldine Marshall Gutfreund is the author of several books on science for children, as well as a novel for teenagers. She has also written many stories, articles, and poems that have appeared in magazines in the United States and in Australia.

She has a degree in zoology from the University of Kentucky, and lives in Paducah, Kentucky, with her husband, Mark, their daughters, Audrey and Rachel, a dachshund dog named Newton, a gerbil named Berry, and two hermit crabs named Pawley and Kermit.